PRIMARY SOURCES IN AMERICAN HISTORY™

GRANT AND LEE AT APPOMATTOX
A PRIMARY SOURCE HISTORY OF THE END OF THE CIVIL WAR

GILLIAN HOUGHTON

rosen central
Primary Source™

The Rosen Publishing Group, Inc., New York

Published in 2004 by The Rosen Publishing Group, Inc.
29 East 21st Street, New York, NY 10010

Library of Congress Cataloging-in-Publication Data

Houghton, Gillian.
Grant and Lee at Appomattox : a primary source history of the end of the Civil War / Gillian Houghton.— 1st ed.
    p. cm. — (Primary sources in American history)
Summary: Examines the events and key figures behind the last campaigns of the Civil War and Robert E. Lee's surrender to the Union forces of Ulysses S. Grant at Appomattox Court House. Includes bibliographical references and index.
ISBN 0-8239-4004-7 (library binding)
1. United States—History—Civil War, 1861-1865—Campaigns—Juvenile literature. 2. United States—History—Civil War, 1861-1865—Campaigns—Sources—Juvenile literature. 3. Lee, Robert E. (Robert Edward), 1807-1870—Juvenile literature. 4. Grant, Ulysses S. (Ulysses Simpson), 1822-1885—Juvenile literature. [1. United States—History—Civil War, 1861-1865—Campaigns. 2. Lee, Robert E. (Robert Edward), 1807-1870. 3. Grant, Ulysses S. (Ulysses Simpson), 1822-1885.] I. Title. II. Series.
E470.H78 2003
973.7'3—dc21
                                                                                2002156099

Manufactured in the United States of America

On the front cover: A painting entitled *The Surrender, Appomattox Court House, Virginia— April 9, 1865*, by Keith Rocco. Courtesy of the National Park Service.

On the back cover: First row (left to right): Immigrants arriving at Ellis Island; Generals Lee and Grant meet to discuss terms of Confederate surrender at Appomattox, Virginia. Second row (left to right): Lewis and Clark meeting with a western Native American tribe during the expedition of the Corps of Discovery; Napoléon at the signing of the Louisiana Purchase. Third row (left to right): Cherokees traveling along the Trail of Tears during their forced relocation west of the Mississippi River; escaped slaves traveling on the Underground Railroad.

Contents

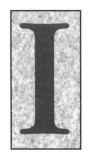

INTRODUCTION

"TO BIND UP THE NATION'S WOUNDS"

"What a cruel thing is war," Confederate general Robert E. Lee wrote to his wife on Christmas Day, 1862. "To separate and destroy families and friends. To fill our hearts with hatred instead of love for our neighbors and to devastate the fair face of this beautiful world." Even crueler is civil war, in which brother is set against brother, countryman against fellow countryman. Beginning on April 12, 1861, the United States was violently torn in two by a four-year-long civil war that pitted the Southern states of the Confederacy (which had seceded, or separated from, from the rest of the country) against the Northern troops of the remaining Union.

Lee was a quiet, dignified commander and a thoughtful man. He was also a relentless, determined soldier, however, and a man who led wave after wave of Confederate troops to the battlefield in their war against the forces of the Union. In the spring of 1864, Lee's Army of Northern Virginia met an equally able and determined foe, General Ulysses S. Grant's Army of the Potomac.

In the North, the inconsistent public support that had fitfully buoyed the war effort for more than three years was again on the wane, due mainly to the staggering loss of life among Union soldiers. In the South, men and supplies were running out. For more

Jefferson Davis *(left; c. 1865)* was the first and last president of the Confederate States of America. He was born in Kentucky in 1808, one year before Abraham Lincoln *(right; c. 1860)*, who was also born in that state. Viewing the South as a "country within a country," Davis was a compromise candidate for president of the Confederacy, just as Lincoln was not the first choice of his Republican Party for the U.S. presidency. Captured a month after Lincoln's assassination in 1865, Davis served two years in prison for treason but was eventually released without trial. He led a quiet life as a private businessman and author until his death in 1889.

than a year, the two generals led their troops in a series of bloody battles, as both armies headed south from the Rappahannock River. Grant was driving his forces to the rebel capital of Richmond, Virginia, in a mad dash to bring an end to the war. Lee, outnumbered and ill equipped, was forced to retreat south and west to keep the hope of a Confederate victory alive. His troops dwindled, but their commitment never flagged.

After more than a year of daily combat with General Grant's army and four long years of civil war, General Lee surrendered to save what was left of his brave forces and his battered country. On April 9, 1865, he and Grant agreed to the conditions of a formal surrender in the Appomattox, Virginia, home of Wilmer McLean. In one brave gesture, Lee halted further bloodshed between fellow Americans and changed the course of history.

With equal care and grace, Grant also rose to the occasion. At the close of the war, Grant shared with Union president Abraham Lincoln the dilemma of reuniting the divided country. Many Unionists clamored for revenge against the Southern rebels. Newspaper editorials called for the humiliation and execution of Confederate soldiers, especially Robert E. Lee. Giddy Union soldiers destroyed the property of Confederate civilians, while many of their commanders called for the total destruction of towns and cities. Lincoln, however, was a firm believer that the future strength of the Union depended on forgiveness.

In his second inaugural address, delivered about six weeks before the Confederate surrender, Lincoln implored his Unionist audience, "With malice toward none; with charity for all; with firmness in the right, as God gives us to see the right, let us strive to finish the work we are in; to bind up the nation's wounds; to care for him who shall have borne the battle ... to do all which may achieve

Bacon's Military Map of America, published in London in August 1862 by Bacon and Company, provides a graphic illustration of a nation torn in two and at war with itself. The free states of the North are colored green, while the Confederate states are pink. Border slave states are colored yellow. Also included are towns, railroads, and the names and boundaries of the states and territories that had begun waging war with each other the year before this map was published.

and cherish a just and lasting peace" (as quoted in Jay Winik's book *April 1865*). Lincoln's message was not lost on Grant, who entered Wilmer McLean's farmhouse with a mixture of reverence and pity for his defeated foe. After a year of intensive, bloody, and near-constant combat against each other's forces, Grant and Lee suddenly found themselves talking politely and quietly together in McLean's parlor. Their subdued, respectful conversation went a long way toward making Lincoln's dream of a peaceful, brotherly, restored union come true.

TIMELINE

January 19, 1807 — Robert E. Lee is born.

April 27, 1822 — Ulysses S. Grant is born.

November 1860 — Abraham Lincoln is elected president of the United States.

December 20, 1860 — South Carolina secedes from the United States, the first of eleven states to do so.

April 12, 1861 — Confederate bombardment of the Union installment at Fort Sumter begins.

April 1861 — Lee is made commander of the Army of Northern Virginia.

March 1864 — Grant is made lieutenant general, commander of Union armies.

May 5–6, 1864 — The Wilderness campaign is waged.

May 8–12, 1864 — The Battle at Spotsylvania is fought.

June 1864– April 2, 1865 — The Union army lays seige to Petersburg.

April 1, 1865 — The Union is victorious at Five Forks.

TIMELINE

April 2, 1865	The Confederate evacuation of Richmond, Virginia, is announced and begun.
April 9, 1865	Lee's army charges the Federal lines near Appomattox Court House and is defeated; Grant and Lee meet at Wilmer McLean's nearby home to negotiate the terms of surrender.
April 12, 1865	The formal surrender of Lee's Army of Northern Virginia is announced.
April 14–15, 1865	Lincoln is assassinated by John Wilkes Booth; Andrew Johnson is sworn in as president.
May 1865	Confederate president Jefferson Davis is captured and imprisoned.
November 1868	Grant is elected president of the United States.
October 12, 1870	Robert E. Lee dies.
November 1872	Grant is reelected president.
July 23, 1885	Ulysses S. Grant dies.

CHAPTER 1

The causes of the rift between the North and the South that led to the Civil War were many and involved a clash of economics, culture, and, according to some observers at the time, even personality. The issues of states' rights (how much independence a state had) and slavery erupted in the sharpest conflicts.

A HOUSE DIVIDED

These issues had troubled the country ever since the founding fathers grappled with them at the Constitutional Convention of 1787. They continued to do so long after the U.S. Constitution was drawn up and signed, and they dramatically converged in the presidential election of 1860.

Mutual Dependence, Diverging Paths

When the delegates met in Philadelphia in 1787 to construct a framework of government for the new nation, five states had already outlawed slavery. Yet fifteen of the fifty-five delegates were slave owners. An additional fifteen representatives profited personally from the South's slave economy. The rest of the delegates, as citizens of a country that proclaimed itself dedicated to the principle that all people are created equal, were implicated in the moral conflict of the so-called peculiar institution of slavery. In the course of the convention's proceedings, however, the issue of slavery was avoided and ignored. Compromises were made in order to preserve the harmony between the states and to create a strong nation.

A slave family stands beside the cotton they have picked in a field near Savannah, Georgia, sometime around 1860. Slaves worked in the fields from the first light of day until dark with a 10-minute lunch break. A slave could not leave the field until an order was given by the slave driver (an overseer). If slaves did not pick the amount of cotton they usually did, they would often be whipped. After a long day laboring in the cotton fields, slaves often returned to their cabins only to perform more chores, including feeding animals, chopping wood, cooking, and cleaning.

As the country galloped into the nineteenth century, the South and the North prospered together, each dependent on the other for economic success. The South's production of cotton had sparked the development of the North's textile industry. Sprawling plantations, worked by an ever growing number of African slaves, dotted the South. Busy urban manufacturing centers and bustling harbors crowded the northeastern seaboard, poised to receive raw cotton and transform it into clothing and linens.

Despite this mutual dependence and trade, however, the North and South would grow along very different lines and develop increasingly distinct social and political identities. The two sides would come to view the nature of the federal government and the states' roles and independence within it very differently. Most important, the South's agricultural economy, which benefited from the free labor of slavery, would come into increasingly sharp conflict with the liberal and humanist ideals of the North's merchant class and Protestant reformers.

These emerging regional differences would lead to growing debate, then to secession, and finally to an extremely violent civil war.

Secessionism

In the late 1850s, seeing the political tide turning against them, the slaveholding upper class of the South threatened to secede and form a new nation, arguing that the federal government had been created and empowered by the states for the mutual benefit of the states. The states had not been created to serve the government but instead were independent and free to pursue their own best interests. The South's best interests, it was argued, lay in the continued use of slave labor. Secessionists claimed that

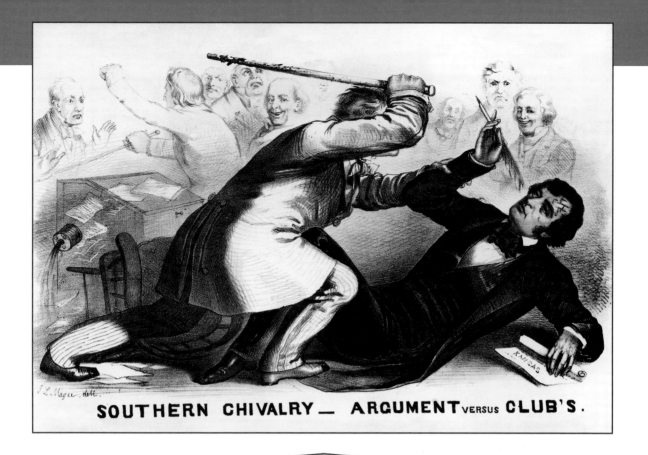

SOUTHERN CHIVALRY — ARGUMENT VERSUS CLUB'S.

This political cartoon from 1856 depicts the attack on Massachusetts senator Charles Sumner by Preston Books, a representative from South Carolina on the floor of the Senate, on May 22, 1856. During a two-day speech he delivered criticizing the South's desire to expand slavery into Kansas, Sumner offended Brooks by apparently insulting Brooks's uncle, Senator Andrew Butler. Brooks used his cane to beat Sumner unconscious. The caning of Sumner became a symbol in the North of Southern brutality and provided the entire nation with a graphic confirmation of the violent rift dividing the nation. In the South, however, Brooks became a hero for seeming to defend Southern honor.

each state had the authority to dissolve the political contract known as the U.S. Constitution.

Unionists, on the other hand, argued that the American people, not the states, had created the nation and that only the people as a whole possessed the power to dissolve the Constitution. These

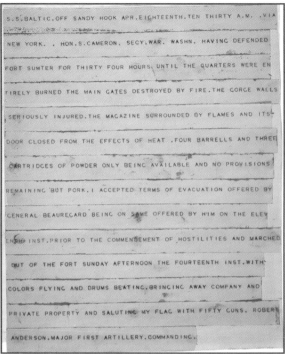

On April 10, 1861, Brigadier General Pierre G.T. Beauregard, commander of the Confederate forces at Charleston, South Carolina, demanded the surrender of the U.S. garrison of Fort Sumter in Charleston Harbor. The garrison's commander, Major Robert Anderson, refused Beauregard's request. On April 12, Confederate guns opened fire on the fort, as pictured above. By 2:30 PM the next day, Major Anderson surrendered Fort Sumter and evacuated the garrison on the following day. A telegram dated April 18, 1861, from him to his superior announcing the surrender appears at top right. The bombardment of Fort Sumter was the first battle of the Civil War. See transcript on page 54.

pro-Union sentiments were expressed in the Republican presidential platform of 1860 and embodied by that party's candidate for president, a lawyer and former senator from Illinois named Abraham Lincoln.

Lincoln was an unpromising candidate for president. He had been defeated in a recent Senate race and was his party's second choice. He ran against a deeply divided Democratic Party, however, which included a large pro-slavery Southern faction. Northern Democrats favored Illinois senator Stephen A. Douglas (who was more interested in preserving the union than abolishing slavery), while Southern Democrats nominated Kentucky senator John C. Breckinridge. A third Democratic candidate, John Bell of Tennessee, led yet another splinter group.

With the Republican Party largely unified in support of him, Lincoln won a substantial minority of the popular vote and outpolled each of his three Democratic opponents. He had won the election, but the majority of the country had voted against him. The political cost of the Republicans' victory would be steep. Lincoln won the presidency but lost the South. In reporting the news of the election, the *Charleston Mercury* compared the secessionists of the South to the colonial revolutionaries of the Boston Tea Party. "The tea has been thrown overboard," the newspaper editorialized. "The revolution of 1860 has been initiated."

On December 20, 1860, South Carolina seceded from the United States, the first of eleven states to do so. On April 12, 1861, General Pierre Beauregard launched the Confederate bombardment of the Union installment at Fort Sumter, in the harbor of Charleston, South Carolina. Thirty-four hours later, the federal troops surrendered the fort. The Civil War had begun.

CHAPTER 2

GRANT AND LEE

The two generals who would face each other across the bloody national divide were a study in contrasts. One had a reputation as a lazy failure and a drunk, a mediocre student, and a poor soldier. The other hailed from one of America's noblest families and distinguished himself from the moment he entered the military academy. One was small, slight, and solitary; the other tall, dashing, and high-spirited. Together, these two very different men would oversee the near destruction of the nation. Together, too, they would begin the long process of healing its violent rift.

Ulysses S. Grant

When civil war broke out and the call for Union soldiers was made in 1861, Ulysses S. Grant announced, "There are but two parties now, traitors and patriots, and I want hereafter to be ranked with the latter." Up to that point, Grant, born Hiram Ulysses Grant, had lived a life characterized by misfortune and failure.

In 1839, Grant's father, Jesse, a successful businessman, arranged for his short and skinny son to attend West Point Military Academy. Young Hiram was mistakenly enrolled under the name Ulysses Simpson Grant, an error that he did not bother to correct. He was a talented horseman but otherwise unfit for cadet life. Grant was painfully shy, preferred reading novels to

In this photograph from 1864–1865, Lieutenant General Ulysses S. Grant leans against a tree outside his tent at his military headquarters in City Point, Virginia. Grant had received his commission as lieutenant general from President Lincoln on March 9, 1864. This promotion represented a stunning turnaround from his undistinguished West Point career and early days as a second lieutenant. The undated inset daguerreotype (an early kind of photograph) shows Lieutenant Grant soon after his graduation from West Point.

studying military tactics, and was unsuited to the academy's strict discipline. He prayed that Congress would abolish the academy and save him from a career in the army. Grant graduated an unimpressive twenty-first in a class of thirty-nine. He went on to serve in the Mexican-American War and came to be considered a good but not great officer. In 1848, he married Julia Dent, with whom he would have four children. When he was assigned to a military outpost in California, however, he was forced to leave his new family behind, unable to pay for their passage west.

Lonely, depressed, and bored, Grant turned to alcohol. Several of the business ventures he ran on the side while serving in the army failed. His health grew poor. In 1854, he was discovered drunk on duty. Given the choice to resign or face trial before a military court, Grant resigned. He returned east, borrowed a plot of Missouri farmland from his father-in-law, and became a planter. Hardscrabble Farm, as Grant humorously named it, was a complete failure, and Julia's father would offer no more aid to his unlucky son-in-law. Grant found work as a bill collector, a real estate agent, and a street vendor. Finally, he took a job as a clerk in his father's Galena, Illinois, leather store. For a modest salary, Grant worked very little and was considered lazy and undisciplined.

Then came the war, about which Grant was uncharacteristically passionate. Grant had finally found his cause. He discovered a sense of purpose and a new focus. Grant enthusiastically sought a command, but his initial requests were ignored by federal officials. Finally, the governor of Illinois found a place for him as a colonel in an Illinois volunteer regiment. Grant quickly gained national recognition for his victories in battles in Belmont, Missouri (1861), and Fort Henry and Fort Donelson (1862), both in Tennessee. For his efforts, Grant was soon promoted. He then

This is a letter dated February 29, 1864, from President Abraham Lincoln to the U.S. Senate in which he nominates Major General Ulysses S. Grant to the position of lieutenant general in the U.S. Army. He was only the second man to ever hold this rank; George Washington was the first. This promotion made Grant the supreme commander of all of the armies of the United States. See transcription on page 54.

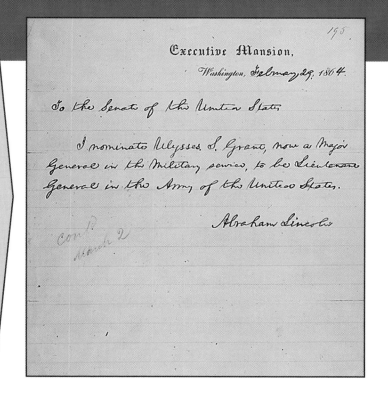

defeated the rebels at Vicksburg, Mississippi, and Chattanooga, Tennessee (both in 1863). In the spring of 1864, he was made commander in chief of the Union army.

The hopes of the Union were pinned on Grant, but he was an unlikely hero. For one, he did not look the part. He stood only 5'8" and was hunchbacked, unpolished, and often sloppy in appearance. He did not have a taste for the pomp of military parades or the songs of the regimental band. Even as a lieutenant general, a rank previously held only by George Washington, Grant wore the uniform of a private. He seemed to long for a quiet, anonymous life with his wife, whom he adored. Military camps filled him with an oppressive sense of loneliness.

Grant's reputation was also hindered by his abuse of alcohol and his unflinching willingness to continuously send fresh Union soldiers onto the killing fields. Ultimately, however, he was respected for his resilience and resolve. While the public's opinion of Grant shifted from admiration to contempt to outright hatred and back again, Grant understood that the unavoidable nature of war was death and destruction. Though he was not insensitive to the tragedies of battle, he would not let his determination to win the war falter. According to Jay Winik, during the Wilderness campaign of 1864, Grant said "Whatever happens, we will not retreat."

Robert E. Lee

Robert E. Lee was a man divided. He was a unionist, but first and foremost, he was a Virginian. His family had famously fought to create and defend the United States since the country's conception. Two of Lee's ancestors had signed the Declaration of Independence. His father, Henry "Lighthorse Harry" Lee, was a Revolutionary War hero, a passionate supporter of a strong centralized government, and the commander of the federal troops deployed to put down the 1794 Whiskey Rebellion, the nation's first encounter with secessionism. However, the Lees were also one of the first families of Virginia, bound to the state's proud history as the home of George Washington, Thomas Jefferson, and, some claimed, freedom itself. In the Lee family, state and regional loyalties ran deep.

Robert E. Lee was born in 1807 at Stratford, a fine brick house on the shore of the Potomac River. The Lees were privileged and well connected, but that would soon change. When Robert was only six years old, his father abandoned the family. Addicted to land speculation (the buying of unused or overlooked property in the hope that it will be developed and increase in value), Harry Lee fled to the West Indies to escape his creditors and his increasingly bad reputation. His scandalous legacy would haunt his sons. The task of redeeming the family's reputation came to rest on Robert's shoulders, and he rose to the challenge.

As a colonel of the 1st U.S. Cavalry Regiment *(inset)*, Robert E. Lee helped put down John Brown's abolitionist rebellion at Harpers Ferry, Virginia. When the Southern states began seceding from the Union, however, Lee refused an offer to take command of the U.S. Army and resigned his commission. Instead he became a general in the Confederate Army, as he is pictured here atop his horse Traveler. Traveler would outlive Lee and walk behind his funeral hearse in 1870. They are buried yards away from each other in Lexington, Virginia.

At the age of eighteen, Robert E. Lee enrolled in West Point and graduated second in his class four years later. In 1831, he married Mary Custis, Martha Washington's great-granddaughter and George Washington's adopted heir. In the person of his wife, Lee found a woman who shared his views on slavery, which Lee deemed as a moral evil, and secessionism, which Lee considered contrary to the spirit of the Constitution.

Lee earned a position in the elite Corps of Engineers, fought valiantly in the Mexican-American War of 1846–1848, served as superintendent of West Point, and commanded the federal troops that put down John Brown's 1859 abolitionist raid of Harpers Ferry, Virginia.

Lee was a striking man who stood nearly six feet tall. He was a notorious flirt, an enthusiastic dancer, and a hearty eater. Yet he was also brooding, moody, and highly emotional. Though fiercely determined in battle, he was capable of publicly weeping over the death of one of his officers. He was an eager scholar of military history and strategy, a resourceful leader, and an ingenious tactician. His skill and service were enthusiastically praised by his commander, Winfield Scott, who said, "If . . . the President of the United States would tell me that a great battle was to be fought for the liberty or slavery of the country, and asked my judgment as to the ability of the commander, I would say with my dying breath, 'Let it be Robert E. Lee!'" (as quoted by Geoffrey C. Ward in his book *The Civil War*).

Four days after the Federal surrender of Fort Sumter, Winfield Scott offered Lee the command of the Union army. Lee felt obliged to refuse and resign his commission. "I cannot raise my hand against my birthplace, my home, my children," he said

In a letter preserved in the National Archives, dated April 20, 1861, and addressed to Simon Cameron, U.S. secretary of war, Robert E. Lee resigns his commission as Colonel of the 1st U.S. Cavalry Regiment. Lee resigned just a week after the Confederate attack on Fort Sumter and the Union surrender of it and four days after he rejected the command of all U.S. armies offered to him by Union general Winfield Scott. By June of the following year, he would command the Army of Northern Virginia. For a complete transcription of Lee's letter of resignation to Secretary Cameron, see page 54.

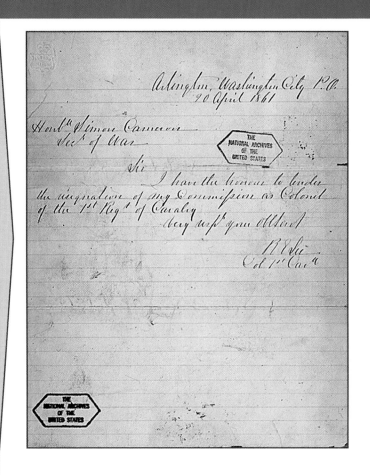

mournfully (according to Jay Winik in *April 1865*). Instead he took command of the Army of Northern Virginia and was promoted to brigadier general in the army of the Confederacy. With Mary Lee settled in the new Confederate capital at Richmond, Virginia, Robert E. Lee went off to war.

CHAPTER 3

At first glance, the rural, agrarian South would have seemed to be able to offer little resistance to the assault of the Federal troops from the more industrialized, densely populated North. On paper, the war looked like it would be a terrible mismatch that would end quickly with a minimum of bloodshed. On the ground, however, a very different and far bloodier story was about to be told.

THE GRIM REALITY OF WAR

Struggling for Advantage

Contrary to popular opinion, the South of 1860 was not entirely unprepared to meet the troops of the mighty, industrialized North. It is true that the North possessed 110,000 manufacturing facilities compared to the South's 18,000. The North, though encompassing only 670,000 square miles of land, was covered with 22,000 miles of railroad, while the South, with a total area of 780,000 square miles, had only 9,000 miles of track. The North boasted a population of 20 million compared to the South's 9 million. All in all, the North was far better equipped than the South to produce, transport, and operate the instruments of war, among them weapons, ammunition, food, blankets, and soldiers.

The South, however, was not without its advantages. Chief among these were Southerners' passionate faith in their cause, a strong communal identity, and an intimate familiarity with the

On May 20, 1864, a day after the twelve-day-long Battle of Spotsylvania finally came to an end, photographer Timothy H. O'Sullivan took this picture of a Confederate soldier awaiting burial. Both sides suffered heavy casualties in the battle, and neither side gained any real advantage. The Confederate Army lost 9,000 to 10,000 men (roughly one out of six soldiers), while the Union lost almost 18,000 (roughly one out of five men).

land upon which the war would be fought, which included dense forests, vast swamps, and steep mountain passes. These strengths would allow the Southerners—Confederate soldiers and civilians alike—to sustain the war far longer than many in the North had expected.

A New Kind of Warfare

At the beginning of the Civil War, American military technology and strategy had changed little since the time of the American Revolution. Generals of the North and the South were taught to engage the enemy in close hand-to-hand combat on flat, wide-open ground, such as farm fields. Equipped with muskets with attached bayonets (inaccurate weapons that took several seconds to load and fire a single shot), foot soldiers were commanded to charge a line of defenders in a solid, orderly mass.

The similarly equipped defensive line might have time to fire their muskets only once or twice between the time when the enemy came into range and when the enemy was directly upon them. The charging troops would suffer only minor losses before reaching the defenders and attacking them by hand. If the invading army outnumbered its opponent, these kinds of battles would continue until the defenders ran out of troops, and then the war would end.

By the middle of the Civil War, however, soldiers were generally equipped with rifles, and this strategy no longer worked. Rifles were accurate up to much greater distances, which meant that charging troops were in danger of being hit long before they reached the defenses of their opponents. In addition, the art of trench warfare was introduced as a defensive strategy by Confederate forces in the spring of 1864 during the Atlanta and Petersburg campaigns. Defensive troops no longer

This photograph, taken around 1860, is entitled *Cannon on Wheels*. Both Union and Confederate forces developed these railroad batteries that allowed them to transport and position heavy artillery for the bombardment of enemy cities and other strategic locations. Some of these artillery pieces weighed as much as 17,000 pounds (7,711 kg) and fired 200-pound (91-kg) shells a distance of three miles (5 km) or more.

stood or crouched on flat land in plain view. Instead, they dug miles of deep ditches, creating a protected maze of highways and byways for secretive defensive movement. From these trenches, soldiers could fire upon their enemies while exposing very little of their bodies to return fire. Used together, the rifle and the defensive trench were virtually unbeatable.

If traditional offensive tactics could not penetrate the entrenched defenses of the Confederate army, Union soldiers would have to find another way to attack them. They would be forced to circle around and launch an assault from the rebels' rear or wage predawn assaults on weak points in the defensive line. They would have to catch the rebel troops on the march or sever their supply lines and starve them.

This new warfare would not be so easy to wage, however. Geography was the Union troops' first obstacle. Union commanders had little and often inaccurate information about the land on which they were fighting, whereas the Confederate troops were familiar with the terrain. The South was not an orderly patchwork of roads and farms, encircling regularly organized towns and cities. Much of the fighting took place in the lush, overgrown forests, along the swollen rivers, and off of the unmapped dirt roads of Virginia and the Carolinas. In the winters, heavy rains flooded the rivers and roads, turning the field of battle into a muddy mess. In the summers, the scorching heat cracked the ground and sent clouds of thick dust into the air, signaling the advance of the marching Union soldiers.

Union generals were prepared for a traditional war of panoramic battles, in which they could sit at a distance and watch the ebb and flow of their troops across a large flat battlefield. Instead, they encountered a dense wilderness. A general could not retreat to a nearby hilltop, observe the battle in progress, and sketch out his next move. Instead, the fighting surrounded and engulfed them. Their sight lines obscured by trees and tangled vegetation, soldiers could see for only a few feet in any direction. The enemy was all but invisible.

Mounting Losses

Sustaining heavy losses while adapting to this new kind of war, the generals of the Union Army of the Potomac stubbornly continued marching south throughout the first three years of the conflict, trying to press ever onward to the Confederate capital of Richmond. The death toll was heartbreaking. On May 5 and 6, 1864, in northern Virginia, in a tangled thicket of trees and creeks known as the Wilderness, General Grant's army lost 17,500 men in just two days of combat against Lee's forces. The Confederate soldiers had begun the battle outnumbered nearly three to one.

This shocking defeat was an ominous sign of things to come for the Union forces in the coming year, the final one of the war. During the next few months, the two armies would meet at the bloody but inconclusive battles of Spotsylvania, North Anna, and Cold Harbor (all in Virginia). Union and Confederate losses ran extremely high in these battles, but neither army gained much of an advantage. When either side ran out of ammunition, they would hurl their bayoneted rifles like spears into the enemy lines and use their regimental flagpoles as weapons.

Neither army would back down, retreat, or surrender. Grant, sensing that the end of the war was near despite his recent heavy losses, pushed mercilessly southward. Lee's determined Confederates dug in their heels, however, refusing to surrender the wilderness below the Rapidan River, which runs east through central Virginia from the Blue Ridge Mountains to the Atlantic Ocean.

Life During Wartime

By March 1865, the Confederate Army of Northern Virginia was on its last legs. Lee's men were living in a thirty-seven-mile-long maze of trenches extending south from Richmond and turning southwest at Petersburg. For nine months, the Confederates had been trapped, capable of rebuffing Grant's daily attacks but unable to defeat the Union troops entirely. While Grant's army was fed and clothed by the well-stocked Union storehouses in nearby City Point, Lee's men were cut off from food, medical aid, blankets, and other basic supplies. The men suffered from poor nutrition and filthy living conditions, succumbing to scurvy, night blindness, and dysentery. Recovering from the most minor wounds was extremely difficult because the unsanitary conditions led to infections.

Soldiers fought over horse dung, in which they would search for undigested corn to add to their meager rations. The soldiers were covered with open sores. Their gums bled, and their teeth fell out. They were little more than skin and bones, and many were unable to rise in the morning, sick with fatigue and weak with fever. Many men were driven to the brink of insanity. While Grant's forces were replenished with a seemingly unending supply of fresh soldiers and grew to 125,000 men, Lee's troops dwindled, eventually numbering only 35,000. Sixty thousand Confederate soldiers had deserted Lee's ranks, finally beaten by the horrific conditions of war.

The Retreat from Richmond

In the early days of March 1865, Lee gathered his officers and devised a final war plan. Withdrawing its troops from Richmond, the Army of Northern Virginia would consolidate and preserve its strength, safely slip away from its Petersburg trenches, and move southwest toward Danville, Virginia. At Danville, it would slip over the Roanoke River and continue south to join Confederate general Joseph E. Johnston in North Carolina for an attack on Union general William Tecumseh Sherman's forces. The plan would have to wait until late March when the roads, muddied by a long winter of rain and snow, would again be dry.

Lee pored over the plans for retreat, establishing alternate escape routes and coordinating the movements of supplies, weapons, official documents, men, and animals. The plan for Lee's army to travel 140 miles to the tiny hamlet of Amelia Court House, where desperately needed food and supplies from Confederate warehouses would await them. Lee's army would regroup and revive themselves before moving on to meet Joe Johnston's troops.

General Grant knew that the time to strike was at hand. Lee's troops were battered and broken, and preoccupied by their preparations for a massive retreat. Grant sent small fighting

In the spring of 1864, General Lee's troops began to dwindle due to death, disease, desertion, starvation, and fatigue. Meanwhile, General Grant's Union forces continued to gain strength as they marched south toward the Confederate headquarters of Richmond, Virginia, and the nearby stronghold of Petersburg *(pictured at top)*. As a result, Petersburg fell to a ten-month-long Union siege on April 2, 1865. The above picture shows a Confederate soldier killed during the siege and left lying in one of the many trenches built around Petersburg.

forces to test Lee's lines at Lewis's Farm, Five Forks, and Dinwiddie Court House. At each skirmish, the Confederates successfully repelled the Union attack. In doing so, however, they extended their defensive lines farther south and west, stretching the resources of an already overburdened army. This was exactly what Grant had hoped would happen.

On April 1, Grant ordered Major General Philip Sheridan to launch a massive attack on Five Forks, a key Confederate post on the road to North Carolina. To preserve their route of retreat, the Confederates would have to save Five Forks. As the bombardment began, the rebels appeared secure in their position, but by the end of the day their fortunes turned, and Five Forks had fallen. Grant, encouraged by the victory, ordered a direct attack on Lee's Petersburg trenches, which began in the early hours of April 2. The Union's cannons sounded, pounding the Confederate trenches for several hours. Before dawn, the Union infantry charged the battered defenders. The two sides fought for eighteen solid hours. In the end, Grant occupied Five Forks, Lee's southernmost regiments had been crushed, and Union soldiers had nearly encircled the Confederate trenches at Petersburg. In a single day, Lee had lost nearly a quarter of his remaining army.

Grant's victorious army marched on to Lee's headquarters at Edge Hill. Lee initially resisted the Union approach. As April 2 wore on, however, he was forced to evacuate his office at Turnbull Hall. As he rode off to the surrounded rebel camp at Petersburg, he watched the building that had housed his office burn.

Lee hoped to lead his men to safety under the cover of night, but when he arrived in Petersburg he discovered that the railroad had been seized, the rebel line had been pushed back again, and the Confederate army's desperate hope for reinforcements had

A sketch by Alfred Waud depicts the fierce battle at Five Forks that took place on April 1, 1865, between the Union infantry and cavalry led by Major General Philip Sheridan and a much smaller Confederate force led by General George Pickett. Sheridan hoped to capture Five Forks and cut one of the Confederacy's few remaining supply lines. The battle lasted only about an hour, and 2,000 to 2,400 Confederate soldiers were quickly captured. In exchange for their weapons, they were offered rations.

gone unfulfilled. Yet he managed to evade Grant once again, sneaking across the Appomattox River that night and galloping west toward Amelia Court House. Grant, who had written triumphantly to his wife to announce the Confederate defeat at Five Forks, refused to see Lee slip away yet again. He set off in hot pursuit, determined to bring an end to the terrible conflict. He knew that he had almost every tactical advantage, and he was determined to win.

CHAPTER 4

On the morning of April 2, 1865, a courier rushed into Saint Paul's Episcopal Church in Richmond and handed Confederate president Jefferson Davis an urgent note from Robert E. Lee. Davis broke the seal and read the letter, the eyes of the entire congregation upon him. The color drained from his face, he rose from his seat, and he strode from the sanctuary. The time has come, Lee had written to Davis as the general watched the Union troops approach his headquarters at Edge Hill. The evacuation of Richmond must begin.

"HOUR AFTER HOUR . . . FIGHTING, AND RETREATING"

Word spread throughout the Confederate capital. At the Second Presbyterian Church, the Reverend Moses Hoge's sermon was interrupted by another messenger carrying a note. After reading it, Hoge announced to his congregation, "Brethren, trying times are before us . . . We may never meet again. Go quietly to your homes, and whatever may be in store for us, let us not forget that we are Christian men and women, and may the protection of the Father, the Son, and the Holy Ghost be with you all" (as quoted by Jay Winik in *April 1865*).

The letter pictured above is an order from the Confederate government's General Post Office Department to pack up the Richmond Post Office and move it to Charlotte, North Carolina. Confederate troops and civilians fleeing Richmond set fire to several warehouses in order to prevent Union seizure of food supplies and goods. Rioters and looters also destroyed parts of the city *(as pictured, top)*. See transcription on page 55.

The Fall of Richmond

When an official announcement of evacuation was made at 4 PM that day, the city of Richmond dissolved into frantic chaos. The entire Confederate government moved 140 miles south to Danville aboard freight cars labeled "Treasury Department," "War Department," and so on. Civilians gathered a few precious belongings and crowded the railroad depots and the roads to Lynchburg and points south, anxiously fleeing what they feared would be vengeful, murderous Union troops.

When night came, Richmonders who could not or would not flee their city took to the streets, looting abandoned stores and houses and passing out drunk in the gutters. Mobs roamed the streets, and fights broke out between fellow Confederates. Others locked themselves behind shuttered windows and waited in terror for the enemy to arrive.

The retreating Confederate military presence set about destroying anything that might be of use to the advancing Union army. Rear Admiral Raphael Semmes blew up the ironclad Confederate fleet anchored in the James River. The force of the blast broke windows all over town, and debris pelted the city. The army set fire to the tobacco warehouses, which burned with a ferocious power. In the night, a strong wind picked up and carried the flames from one building to the next. The city, which had been covered in darkness since the gas lines had been shut off earlier in the evening, was soon aglow with the raging fire. Glass, brick, and plaster rained on the streets as block after block fell to the flames. The fire department was helpless; a crazed Confederate mob had destroyed their fire hoses earlier that day.

The rhythmic drumbeat of exploding shells and crumbling buildings continued throughout the night. In the morning,

Richmonders, many of whom found themselves suddenly homeless and penniless, wandered helplessly past dying fires, heaps of rubble, and a forest of freestanding chimneys, the houses having burned or collapsed around them.

Then the Union army came, with its wagons rolling and soldiers marching through the streets of Richmond. Met by the enthusiastic cheers of Richmond's newly emancipated black residents, the Union soldiers set to work mending the railroads, clearing the streets of debris, and providing much needed food to Richmond's civilians. "Exactly at eight o'clock," one Richmond resident wrote, "the Confederate flag that fluttered above the Capitol came down and the Stars and Stripes were run up . . . We covered our faces and cried aloud. All through the house was the sound of sobbing. It was the house of mourning" (according to Geoffrey C. Ward).

Meanwhile, Robert E. Lee was on the run, heading through the nearly impenetrable Virginia countryside due west to Amelia Court House. Ulysses S. Grant was following fast on his heels. As the two armies marched on, regular skirmishes broke out between the lines at the Confederates' rear. Wrote one reporter, "On and on, hour after hour, from hilltop to hilltop, the lines were alternately forming, fighting, and retreating, making one almost continuous battle. A boy soldier came running by at the top of his speed. When asked why he was running, he shouted back, 'I'm running 'cause I can't fly!'" (as quoted by Ward).

Amelia Court House

On April 4, the first of Lee's troops reached Amelia Court House. It was a small, sleepy town, boasting only a handful of shops surrounding a public square. Lee rushed ahead to the rail depot, eager to unpack the desperately needed food he had requested from the commissary (the army's store of equipment and food). His heart sank when he found crate upon crate of ammunition and harnesses, but no food. Thanks to a bureaucratic mistake at Confederate army headquarters, his men would go hungry.

Lee issued an urgent request to the local residents for food and supplies. The last of his troops arrived in the tiny town late in the evening, only to receive the deeply disappointing news that no food awaited them. They refused to be discouraged, however. As Lee rode through the infantry camps that night, his men raised their arms and their voices in support of their general. War whoops rang out in the night, and the hungry but still loyal and faithful men drifted off to sleep.

In the morning, however, there was more bad news. Lee received word that the people of Amelia had no more to give to the Confederate armies. The town had exhausted its supply of meat, milk, and bread. Lee ordered his weary, starving men to march on. Their destination was a town eighteen miles to the south called Burkeville, Virginia. Lee would again request provisions be sent ahead from the new Confederate capital at Danville, Virginia, ninety-six miles farther south.

Yet Grant shadowed Lee's every move and blocked his way. The route of retreat through Burkeville was interrupted by a Federal blockade of earthworks (a barricade made of soil and vegetation), cavalry, and infantry at Jetersville, Virginia. Lee knew he could not budge the Union defenders from their positions. Grant had outmaneuvered him. Lee's only hope lay due west, at Lynchburg. He ordered his men to rise and march once again. Somehow the starved Confederate soldiers found the strength and will to get to their feet and press on.

The Final March

The march to Lynchburg was extremely difficult. Not only were many of Lee's troops starving, sick, shoeless, and virtually senseless, but the terrain was uneven, the roads were muddy, and the weather was fierce as well. Over the course of the march, the sun scorched them, the rain pounded them, and the blustery wind knocked them off their already unsteady feet.

The march continued on through the night, the next day, and the following night. Along the way, Grant's army, under Philip Sheridan, tormented the Confederates with fierce blows to Lee's left flank. Eager to launch a full-scale attack that would stop Lee in his tracks, Grant planned to send his troops in a northwest arc around Lee's troops to charge Confederate front lines.

The opportunity to attack came as the Confederate army neared Sayler's Creek. Union cavalry, led by George Armstrong Custer and followed by artillery and infantry (cannons and foot soldiers), broke through Lee's lines. The two armies met in savage hand-to-hand combat. "I saw numbers of men kill each other with bayonets and the butts of muskets," said one Confederate officer, "and even bite each other's throats and ears and noses, rolling on the ground like wild beasts" (as quoted by Geoffrey C. Ward in *The Civil War*). Soldiers scratched at the eyes of their enemies, kicked each other, and beat each other with their fists. By the end, the rebels were simply outnumbered. Lee had lost 8,000 men to capture or death. Though the rebels raised the cry "Where's the man who won't follow Uncle Robert?" Lee knew that the end was near.

The following morning, Lee's men arrived at Farmville, Virginia, where the first shipment of rations awaited them. Only

the last of Ewells Corps

This 1865 sketch shows Confederate soldiers surrendering to Union forces after the battle of Sayler's Creek, on April 6, 1865. In this battle, the Union army had cut off part of the exhausted and hungry Confederate forces trying to retreat westward from Richmond and Petersburg. A third of General Lee's remaining troops were captured as a result, including Major General George Washington Custis Lee, Robert E. Lee's eldest son.

a portion of the army was able to eat and rest, however, before Lee ordered the men to march on. Grant had closed the gap between the two armies, and fighting had already broken out in the streets of the town.

CHAPTER 5

As the Union army pushed through Farmville, Ulysses S. Grant sat down to write a letter to his Confederate counterpart. At 10 PM that evening, the letter was delivered to Robert E. Lee. As Jay Winik recounts in *April 1865*, Grant offered Lee the opportunity to surrender, noting the "hopelessness of further resistance on the part of the Army of Northern Virginia." Lee responded, "Though not entertaining the opinion you express of the hopelessness of further resistance . . . I reciprocate your desire to avoid the useless effusion of blood, & therefore . . .

SURRENDER

ask the terms you will offer on the condition of [the Confederate army's] surrender."

Lee's response in this and further correspondence between the two generals revealed that his determination to fight on was mingled with growing anxiety. As his battered, bedraggled army continued its retreat, Lee was faced with a difficult decision. Should he stand his ground and watch his men die at their posts, as he had once urged them to do? Should he accept Grant's peace, at whatever cost, and bring a merciful end to the conflict? Or should he continue the retreat to Lynchburg and beyond, leading his men to the safety of the Blue Ridge Mountains where they could launch a new guerrilla-style war?

Guerrilla Warfare

Guerrilla warfare is a type of combat that involves surprise attacks, ambushes, assassinations, harassment, and sabotage. It is usually waged against stronger, better organized forces by so-called irregular armies—groups of people devoted to a cause but not part of any formal military unit. Guerrilla warfare is often the combat strategy of outnumbered soldiers who have an intimate familiarity with local geography and can count on the support of the local population. With their surprise attacks, virtual invisibility, and quick escapes, guerrillas sap their enemy's strength and destroy their morale, often allowing the guerillas to bring down a force much larger than their own.

Lee was familiar with the history of guerrilla warfare and its important role in the Civil War. Confederate guerrilla commanders, most notably John S. Mosby and William Quantrill, had been terrorizing isolated Union communities throughout the Midwest since the first days of the war. The guerrillas sacked and burned villages, tortured and killed pro-Union men and women, struck military encampments when least expected, and pierced Union supply lines. They would then disappear into the darkness and the hills of Missouri, Tennessee, and western Virginia. They were brutal and ruthless, and their equally passionate civilian followers would pick up where they left off.

Already, several units of Lee's army had deserted the front lines and vanished into the hills. These Confederate soldiers were capable of surviving indefinitely in the southern wilderness and determined to fight to the death. Lee's trusted aides and his president, Jefferson Davis, recommended that the rest of Lee's army follow their example.

This is the white linen dish towel that was used as a flag of truce by the staff officer of Confederate general James Longstreet at Appomattox. Under orders from General Lee, Longstreet walked toward the Union cavalry, which was led by General George Custer (who would die in 1876 leading his troops into the Battle of Little Bighorn). Custer's wife, Elizabeth Bacon Custer, later donated the towel to the Smithsonian Institution.

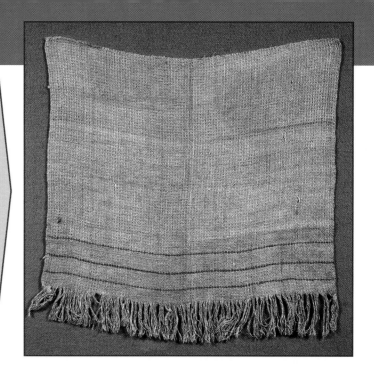

The Last Stand

In the predawn mist of April 9, 1865, Lee's army staged one final charge. The rebels raised their arms and let out a piercing war whoop, then charged the Federal lines, which almost completely surrounded the Confederate encampment near Appomattox Court House. Surprising the Union cavalry, the rebels gained some ground and some enemy artillery. This early success, however, eroded quickly. When they approached the ridge of a nearby hill, they saw two solid miles of Federal infantrymen to their front and a wall of Union soldiers closing in on their rear. At 8 AM, Confederate general John B. Gordon sent word to Lee: There was nothing left for Gordon's troops to do.

Lee called a meeting of his most trusted officers and listened as they counseled him to flee to the hills and prepare the rebels for a guerrilla war. Yet Lee could not agree to a plan he knew would further tear apart the fabric of the nation and take years to mend. In a guerrilla war, Lee argued, "The men would be without rations and under no control of officers . . .

They would be compelled to rob and steal in order to live. They would become . . . bands of marauders" (as quoted by Jay Winik). The desperate guerrillas and the increasingly frustrated Union soldiers sent to fight them would wreak havoc on the country. Lee could not send his men or the United States into such an uncertain future. He would risk whatever vengeful punishment the North would devise for him—a man considered a traitor in the eyes of the Union—and surrender.

Honor in Victory and Defeat

Lee and Grant arranged to meet at 1:30 PM at the home of Wilmer McLean, in the village of Appomattox Court House, the county seat. The sleepy town was dotted with clapboard cottages, several stores, and the county courthouse. Lee was waiting in the parlor of McLean's solid brick house when Grant arrived. The two generals shook hands and took their seats, eight feet apart. Grant was polite and nervous in the presence of the famous General Lee, eagerly rambling on for several minutes while the Confederate general sat silently.

After exchanging some pleasantries, Grant began to lay out his proposed terms of surrender. Confederate officers and soldiers would be paroled but disqualified from future military service. Their arms and ammunition would also be confiscated by the federal government. The terms were just what Lee had hoped for but dared not expect. The Confederates would suffer no humiliation or prosecution at the hands of the Union government. They would not be put on trial for treason. With Lee's approval, Grant committed the terms to paper.

On one point, however, Lee paused. The Confederate cavalry and artillerists, he said, owned their horses; unlike those in the Union army, mounts were not provided by the poorly equipped Confederate army. Therefore, Lee asked Grant to make an exception in this case and allow the soldiers to keep their horses. His war-weary soldiers would soon be returning to their farms and shops, and they would need their horses to get their fields and businesses up and running again.

Grant, initially hesitant, soon accepted Lee's proposal. In doing so, he set the tone and provided the framework for the Union's treatment of its defeated foe. Grant had taken a powerful, symbolic step toward giving the former rebels the tools they would need to rebuild the South and, more important, toward healing the rift between countrymen. A spirit of brotherhood prevailed in Appomattox Court House, a spirit that would spread beyond the tiny village and very gradually draw the shattered nation together again.

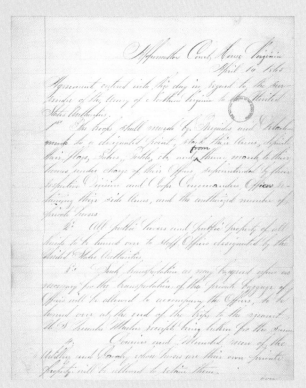

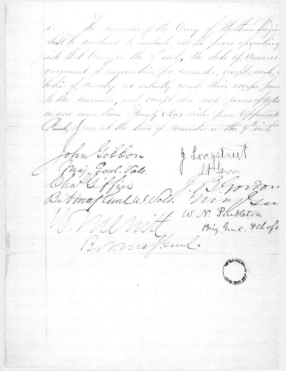

On April 10, 1865, a day after Grant and Lee met in Appomattox to discuss Lee's surrender, this document was drawn up and signed. The agreement basically declared the Confederate soldiers free to return home if they agreed to quit fighting and give up their weapons, even though they were guilty of treason in the Union's eyes. In a formal ceremony two days later, Lee's infantry surrendered their weapons, folded their battle flags, and received their parole papers. See transcription on page 55.

A New Era of Peace and Reconciliation?

The two generals signed the orders of surrender, shook hands, and proceeded out of the house. They mounted their horses and returned to their camps. In the Union camp, the soldiers shouted and danced for joy, regimental bands struck up festive tunes, artillerists fired a gun salute, and infantrymen tossed their knapsacks and hats into the air. Grant did not share in their revelry, however. His thoughts turned to reconciliation and peace. In the weeks and months ahead, Ulysses S. Grant would have to lead his rambunctious men into a new era, one that would require great discipline, calm, and forgiveness. He was solemn in his victory, according to Winik, penning only a brief note to the Union secretary of war, Edwin Stanton: "General Lee surrendered the Army of Northern Virginia this afternoon on terms proposed by myself."

As he entered the Confederate camp, Lee openly wept. Many of his men followed suit, falling to the ground, burying their faces in their hands, and sobbing. Other Confederate soldiers cursed the day's events, vowing to join Joe Johnston's army in North Carolina and fight to the death. Winik claims Lee was virtually speechless, only urging his distraught men, "Go home now, and if you make as good citizens as you have soldiers, you will do well, and I shall always be proud of you."

On April 12, the two armies met again, this time in a formal ceremony of surrender. Over the course of seven hours, each Confederate division paraded by the Union troops, carefully stacked their arms and ammunition, and formally folded their bloodstained regimental flags. As the ceremony commenced, Union officer Joshua L. Chamberlain spontaneously ordered his men to raise their rifles to their shoulders, a gesture of humble respect and honor offered to the defeated Confederates. For

In this 1865 sketch by Alfred Waud, General Robert E. Lee is seen returning to his headquarters from his meeting with General Grant at the McLean house in Appomattox. Lee was said to be greatly loved by his soldiers who, though deeply upset by news of the surrender, nevertheless respectfully took their hats off as he passed by and then cheered him loudly. As he passed his men, tears began streaming down his face, and he was reported to have said, "Men, we have fought through the war together. I have done the best that I could for you."

both sides, it was a somber event that no participant would ever forget. This show of peace and goodwill, however, did not mean that the country's road to reunification would be a smooth or a short one.

CHAPTER 6

T hough the Confederate army had surrendered, the Civil War was not yet at an end. Two Southern state capitals were still occupied by rebel forces. Confederate soldiers, numbering 175,000, were still eager to fight. Guerrilla bands, under John Mosby, William Quantrill, and Nathan Bedford Forrest, were still strong. Rebel commanders, most notably Joe Johnston, still roamed the battlefields of the South.

The thirty days following the surrender were a wild and uncertain time. On April 14—just two days after the Confederate surrender—Abraham Lincoln was assassinated by John Wilkes Booth, while Booth's coconspirators attempted to carry out vicious attacks on the secretary of state, William Seward, and Vice President Andrew Johnson. Lincoln died at 7:22 AM the next day, and Johnson was sworn in as president at 10 AM. Joe Johnston's surrender to William Tecumseh Sherman would take place on April 26, the same day Lincoln's assassin was captured and killed in a tobacco barn in Virginia. In May, a final shock came. Jefferson Davis, who had fled west in hopes of rallying support for the Confederacy in Texas, was captured and imprisoned in Fortress Monroe. Scattered

THE PEACEMAKERS

In this 1870 photograph by D. J. Ryan, Robert E. Lee *(right)* is shown sitting with former Confederate general Joseph E. Johnston five years after the end of the Civil War. After the Confederate surrender at Appomattox, Lee returned to Richmond, Virginia, as a paroled prisoner of war. He was stripped of his U.S. citizenship and indicted for (charged with) treason but never brought to trial. During the last five years of his life, he served as president of Washington College in Lexington, Virginia, where he died on October 12, 1870, of heart disease.

Confederate forces in the West still persisted in fighting, but the war was finally at an end.

Throughout these troubled times, the Union stood firm, in no small part due to the peace that was forged in Wilmer McLean's isolated home and the two gracious, dignified generals who came to represent the agreement. Though Congress refused to pardon him or restore his full citizenship, Robert E. Lee took a renewed oath of allegiance to the United States and urged his fellow Southerners and former Confederate soldiers to do so as well. A model of forgiveness and goodwill, Ward claims, Lee once responded to the complaints of a former Confederate, whose prized tree had been destroyed by Union guns, by saying, "Cut it down, my dear Madam, and forget it."

Lee went on to serve as president of Washington College in Lexington, Virginia, a position he held until his death in 1870. There, several years after the war, a professor made a critical comment about Ulysses S. Grant, to which, according to Ward, Lee replied, "Sir, if you ever again presume to speak disrespectfully of General Grant in my presence, either you or I will sever his connection with this university."

Grant shared Lee's commitment to reunification; he was elected president in 1868 and 1872 and worked tirelessly to restore national unity. He was a strong supporter of amnesty (freedom from prosecution) for former Confederates and civil rights for emancipated slaves. He campaigned in favor of the Force Acts—legislation passed by the government that protected the voting and property rights of former slaves. He took strong steps to stabilize and rebuild the South's economy and the nation's currency as well.

This 1873 Matthew Brady photograph shows President Ulysses S. Grant delivering his inaugural address on the east portico of the U.S. Capitol on March 4, 1873. Following the agonies of the Civil War, the assassination of Lincoln, and the ongoing social dislocations in the postwar United States, the American people hoped that as president the former general would provide stability and an end to turmoil. Instead, his two administrations became embroiled in controversy and charges of corruption and bribery. After the presidency, Grant was diagnosed with throat cancer and began hurriedly writing his memoirs to pay off his debts and provide for his family after his death. Soon after completing them, he died, on July 23, 1885.

Grant's legacy as president is overshadowed, however, by the corruption of his cabinet and fellow Republican party members, who were accused of embezzling (stealing) tax revenue, accepting bribes, and engaging in questionable business practices. When his second term as president ended in 1877, the discouraged politician retired from public life. He spent some time traveling the world before returning to the United States and investing in a Wall Street brokerage firm, where an unscrupulous employee embezzled millions of dollars and sent the Grants into bankruptcy. Penniless and ill, he retired to an upstate New York home, where he would write his memoirs until just before his death in 1885.

Of the struggling United States, Grant wrote in his autobiography, "I feel that we are on the eve of a new era, when there is to be a great harmony between the Federal and Confederate. I cannot stay to be a living witness to this prophecy, but I feel it within me that it is so." While the reconstruction of the Union would be a long and difficult process, and relations between the North and South would continue to be strained well into the twentieth century and the Civil Rights era, many of the country's wounds would heal and the states would become united again. Much of the credit for this reconciliation belongs to the two veteran warriors—Ulysses S. Grant and Robert E. Lee—who proved themselves to be expert peacemakers.

PRIMARY SOURCE TRANSCRIPTIONS

Page 14: Telegram Announcing the Surrender of Fort Sumter from Major Robert Anderson to U.S. Secretary of War Simon Cameron, April 18, 1861

Transcription
S.S. Baltic. Off Sandy Hook Apr. [April] eighteenth. Ten Thirty A.M. Via New York. Hon. [Honorable] S. Cameron, Secy. War. Washn. [Secretary of War, Washington] Having defended Fort Sumter for thirty four hours until the quarters were entirely burned the main gates destroyed by fire. The gorge walls seriously injured. The magazine surrounded by flames and its door closed from the effects of heat. Four barrells and three cartridges of powder only being available and no provisions remaining but pork, I accepted terms of evacuation offered by General Beauregard being on same offered by him on the eleventh inst. [abbreviation for "instant;" meaning "in or of the present month"] prior to the commencement of hostilities and marched out of the fort Sunday afternoon the fourteenth inst. With colors flying and drums beating. Bringing away company and private property and saluting my flag with fifty guns. Robert Anderson. Major First Artillery. Commanding.

Page 19: Letter from President Abraham Lincoln to the U.S. Senate Nominating Ulysses S. Grant To Be Lieutenant General in the U.S. Army, Feb. 29, 1864

Transcription
Executive Mansion,
Washington, February 29, 1864

To the Senate of the United States

I nominate Ulysses S. Grant, now a Major General in the Military service, to be Lieutenant General in the Army of the United States.

Abraham Lincoln

Page 23: Colonel Robert E. Lee's Letter to U.S. Secretary of War Simon Cameron Resigning His Commission, April 20, 1861

Transcription
Arlington, Washington City P.O.
20 April 1861

Honorable Simon Cameron
Sect. Of War

Sir
I have the honour to tender the resignation of my commission as Colonel of the 1st Regt. [Regiment] of Cavalry.
Very respt. Your obt. Servt. [Very respectfully your obedient servant]
R E Lee
Col 1st Cav [Colonel of the First Cavalry]

Page 35: Acting Auditor of the Richmond, Virginia, Post Office Anson Morse's Letter to C. G. Addison Ordering the Removal of the Post Office to Charlotte, North Carolina, April 2, 1865

Transcription
Richmond, VA. April 2, 1865

Mr. C.G. Addison
You are hereby ordered to accompany the books, records &c of this office to Charlotte N.C. and remain there until further orders.

Anson Morse
Acting Auditor

Page 46: The Articles of Agreement Relating to the Surrender of the Army of Northern Virginia to the U.S. Authorities at Appomattox, Virginia, Dated April 10, 1865

Transcription
Appomattox Court House Virginia
April 10, 1865

Agreement entered into this day in regard to the surrender of the Army of Northern Virginia to the United States Authorities.

1st The troops shall march by Brigades and Detachments to a designated point, stock their Arms, deposit their flags, Sabres, Pistols, etc. and from thence march to their homes under charge of their Officers, superintended by their respective Division and Corps Commanders, Officers, retaining their side Arms, and the authorized number of private horses.

2. All public horses and public property of all kinds to be turned over to Staff Officers designated by the United States Authorities.

3. Such transportation as may be agreed upon as necessary for the transportation of the Private baggage of Officers will be allowed to accompany the Officers, to be turned over at the end of the trip to the nearest U.S. Quarter Masters, receipts being taken for the same.

4. Couriers and Wounded men of the artillery and Cavalry whose horses are their own private property will be allowed to retain them.

5. The surrender of the Army of Northern Virginia shall be construed to include all the forces operating with that Army on the 8th inst., the date of commencement of negociation for surrender, except such bodies of Cavalry as actually made their escape previous to the surrender, and except also such forces of Artillery as were more than Twenty (20) miles from Appomattox Court House at the time of Surrender on the 9th inst.

GLOSSARY

abolitionists Men and women who worked to end slavery.

amnesty Granting a pardon to an individual or group.

artillerists Soldiers who fight with large guns or cannons.

bayonet A knife attached to the front end of a rifle.

cavalry A group of soldiers who fight on horseback.

Confederate A person who fought for the South in the Civil War.

Constitutional Convention The political body that met in the summer of 1787 to create the U.S. Constitution.

dysentery A disease marked by severe diarrhea and the passage of mucus and blood.

effusion The flow of fluid.

embezzle To take something for personal use that does not belong to you but that has been entrusted to your care.

guerrilla A small troop of soldiers who use a combat strategy that emphasizes quick raids, hiding out among the local population, and sabotage.

infantry The part of an army that fights on foot.

ironclad Ships covered with iron or steel to protect them from cannons and gunfire.

marauders People who roam about, raiding towns in search of goods to steal.

panoramic Presenting a complete view of a scene.

pomp A show of magnificence.

rations Food given to people in controlled amounts so that supplies will last for a certain amount of time.

reciprocate To offer something of equal value in return for something given.

regiment A grouping of soldiers into a unit within the military.

reinforcements Anything that strengthens, specifically additional troops or warships to make stronger those already sent.

relinquish To give up control of something.

scurvy A disease resulting from a deficiency of vitamin C, characterized by weakness and bleeding from mucous membranes.

secessionists People who want to secede, or withdraw, from a group or country.

treason The crime of planning to overthrow one's own government or kill the leader of one's country.

Unionists People who remained loyal to the federal government during the Civil War.

Whiskey Rebellion A revolt staged by Midwestern farmers against the federal government's tax on whiskey.

FOR MORE INFORMATION

Organizations

Appomattox Court House National Historic Park
Highway 24, P.O. Box 218
Appomattox, VA 24522
(434) 352-8987, extension 26
Web site: http://www.nps.gov/apco

National Civil War Association
P.O. Box 1256
Santa Clara, CA 95052-1256
Web site: http://ncwa.org

National Civil War Museum
1 Lincoln Circle at Reservoir Park
P.O. Box 1861
Harrisburg, PA 17105-1861
(717) 260-1861
Web site: http://www.nationalcivilwarmuseum.org

Virginia Historical Society
428 North Boulevard
Richmond, VA 23220
(804) 358-4901
Web site: http://www.vahistorical.org

Virginia Military Institute Archives
Preston Library
Lexington, VA 24450
(540) 464-7566
Web site: http://www.vmi.edu/archives/cwsource.html

Documentaries
Burns, Ken. *The Civil War*. Directed by Ken Burns. 660 min. PBS,
2002. DVD/VHS.

Web Sites
Due to the changing nature of Internet links, the Rosen
Publishing Group, Inc., has developed an online list of Web
sites related to the subject of this book. This site is updated
regularly. Please use this link to access the list:

http://www.rosenlinks.com/psah/grla

FOR FURTHER READING

Freeman, Douglass Southall. *Lee*. New York: Touchstone Books, 1997.

Grant, Ulysses S. *Personal Memoirs: Ulysses S. Grant*. New York: Modern Library, 1999.

Hakim, Joy. *A History of Us, Book 6: War, Terrible War*. New York: Oxford University Press, 2002.

Ray, Delia. *A Nation Torn: The Story of How the Civil War Began*. New York: Puffin, 1996.

Smith, Cater, ed. *The Road to Appomattox: A Sourcebook on the Civil War*. Brookfield, CT: Millbrook Press, 1995.

Sullivan, George. *Portraits of War: Civil War Photographers and Their Work*. Brookfield, CT: Millbrook Press, 1998.

Ward, Geoffrey C. *The Civil War: An Illustrated History*. New York: Knopf, 1990.

BIBLIOGRAPHY

Catton, Bruce. *A Stillness at Appomattox*. New York: Anchor Books, 1953.

Foote, Shelby. *The Civil War: A Narrative: Fort Sumter to Perryville, Fredericksburg to Meridian, Red River to Appomattox*. New York: Vintage Books, 1986.

Freeman, Douglass Southall. *Lee*. New York: Touchstone Books, 1997.

Grant, Ulysses S. *Personal Memoirs: Ulysses S. Grant*. New York: Modern Library, 1999.

McPherson, James M. *American Heritage New History of the Civil War*. New York: American Heritage, 1996.

Pfanz, Donald C. "The Angel of Marye's Heights." America's Civil War. 2002. Retrieved February 2003. (http://www.fredericksburg.com/Civil War/Battle/0908CW)

Ward, Geoffrey C. *The Civil War: An Illustrated History*. New York: Knopf, 1990.

Winik, Jay. *April 1865: The Month That Saved America*. New York: HarperCollins, 2001.

# PRIMARY SOURCE IMAGE LIST

Page 5 (left): An untitled photograph of Jefferson Davis, c. 1865, by Mathew Brady. Courtesy of the Hulton Archive.

Page 5 (right): An untitled photograph of Abraham Lincoln, c. 1860, by Alexander Gardner. Courtesy of the Hulton Archive.

Page 7: A map entitled "Bacon's Military Map of America," published in London, England, in 1862 by Bacon and Company. Courtesy of the Library of Congress.

Page 11: A photograph entitled "African American Slaves in Cotton Field," taken in Savannah, Georgia, c. 1860. Courtesy of the Corbis Archive.

Page 13: A political cartoon, c. 1856, entitled "Southern Chivalry." Courtesy of the Corbis Archive.

Page 14 (left): A lithograph entitled "The Bombardment of Fort Sumter," by Currier and Ives. Courtesy of the Prints and Photographs Division of the Library of Congress.

Page 14 (right): An April 18, 1861, telegram from Major Robert Anderson to Simon Cameron, secretary of war, announcing the surrender of Fort Sumter. Housed in the National Archives.

Page 17: A stereograph by Mathew Brady entitled "Lieut. Gen. Grant, at his Head Quarters, City Point, VA," taken in August 1864. (A stereograph is a nineteenth-century photographic technique that involves laying two images atop one another, creating a three-dimensional effect.) Courtesy of the Library of Congress.

Page 17 (inset): A c. 1843 daguerreotype entitled "Portrait of U. S. Grant as 2nd Lieutenant." Photographer unknown. Courtesy of the Corbis Archive.

Page 19: A letter dated Feb. 29, 1864, from President Abraham Lincoln to the U.S. Senate nominating Ulysses S. Grant to the position of lieutenant general of the Army of the United States. Housed in the National Archives.

Page 21: An untitled painting (c. 1866-1870) of General Robert E. Lee and his horse Traveler, based upon an original photograph by Michael Miley taken in 1866. Courtesy of Corbis.

Page 21 (inset): An 1861 studio portrait of Robert E. Lee when he was a colonel of the 1st U.S. Cavalry Regiment. Artist unknown. Courtesy of the Corbis Archive.

Page 23: A letter dated April 20, 1861, from Robert E. Lee to the U.S. secretary of war, Simon Cameron, resigning his commission as colonel of the 1st U.S. Cavalry Regiment. Housed in the National Archives.

Page 25: A May 20, 1864, photograph by Timothy H. O'Sullivan of a Confederate soldier killed in the battle of Spotsylvania. Courtesy of the Library of Congress.

Page 27: A c. 1860 photograph entitled Cannon on Wheels. Photographer unknown. Courtesy of the Hulton Archive.

Page 31 (top): An untitled 1864 photograph of the Union army on the move in the spring of 1864. Photographer unknown. Courtesy of the Library of Congress.

Page 31 (bottom): An untitled 1865 photograph of a Confederate soldier killed in a Petersburg trench during the long siege of the town. Courtesy of the Library of Congress.

Page 33: An 1865 sketch by Alfred Waud shows the Union attack on Confederate forces at Five Forks, Virginia. Courtesy of the Library of Congress.

Page 35 (top): An untitled April 1865 photograph of the burnt ruins of Richmond, Virginia, following the Confederate evacuation of the city. Photographer unknown. Courtesy of the Library of Congress.

Page 35 (bottom): A letter dated April 2, 1865, from Anson Morse, acting auditor, to C. G. Addison, ordering the removal of the Richmond, Virginia, post office to Charlotte, North Carolina. Housed in the National Postal Museum, Smithsonian Institution.

Page 40: An 1865 sketch by an unknown artist depicting the surrender of Confederate soldiers following the battle of Sayler's Creek, Virginia. Courtesy of the Hulton Archive.

Page 43: The white linen dish towel used by Confederate general James Longstreet as a flag of truce at Appomattox on April 9, 1865. Housed in the Smithsonian Institution.

Page 44: A c. 1865 photograph by Timothy H. O'Sullivan of Wilmer McLean's house in Appomattox, Virginia, where the terms of a Confederate surrender were discussed between Generals Grant and Lee. Courtesy of Corbis.

Page 46: This is document entitled "Articles of Agreement Relating to the Surrender of the Army of Northern Virginia," dated April 10, 1865. Housed in the National Archives.

Page 48: An untitled 1865 sketch by Alfred Waud depicting General Lee's return to his headquarters following his surrender at Appomattox. Courtesy of the Library of Congress.

Page 50: An 1870 photograph by D. J. Ryan of Robert E. Lee and Joseph E. Johnston. Housed in the National Portrait Gallery of the Smithsonian Institution. Courtesy of Art Resource, New York.

Page 52: An untitled March 4, 1873, Matthew Brady photograph of President Ulysses S. Grant delivering his inaugural address on the east portico of the U.S. Capitol. Courtesy of the Prints and Photographs Division of the Library of Congress.

INDEX

About the Author

Gillian Houghton is an editor and freelance writer in New York City. She has written on a variety of subjects but remains especially interested in nineteenth-century American history.

Photo Credits

Front cover, back cover (top right) National Park Service, artist, Keith Rocco; back cover (top left and bottom right), pp. 14 (left), 25, 33, 48, 52 Library of Congress, Prints and Photographs Division; back cover (middle left) Yale Collection of Western Americana, Beinecke Rare Book and Manuscript Library; back cover (middle right) Louisiana State Museum, gift of Dr. and Mrs. E. Ralph Lupin; back cover (bottom left) Woolaroc Museum, Bartlesville, Oklahoma; pp. 1, 17, 21, 31 (top), 35 (top), 44 © Corbis; p. 5 (left and right), 27, 40 © Hulton/Archive/ Getty Images; p. 7 Library of Congress, Geography and Map Division; pp. 11, 13, 17 (inset) © Bettmann/Corbis; pp. 14 (right), 46 Still Picture Branch, National Archives and Records Administration; p. 19 National Archives and Records Administration; p. 23 Old Military and Civil Records LICON, National Archives and Records Administration; p. 31 (bottom) © Medford Historical Society Collection/Corbis; p. 35 (bottom) National Postal Museum, Smithsonian Institution; p. 43 National Museum of American History, Smithsonian Institution, Behring Center; p. 50 National Portrait Gallery, Smithsonian Institution/Art Resource, New York.

Designer: Nelson Sa; Photo Researcher: Peter Tomlinson